Breakouts Made Easy

Pete Dulany and Haley Kalinichenko

Breakouts Made Easy

ISBN: 1539611469
ISBN-13: 978-1539611462

Printed in the United States of America

First Printing February, 2017.

CONTENTS

ACKNOWLEDGMENTS

Thank you to Lorinda Sankey for your kind heart, loving spirit, and insight as my professor. You've taught me more than content needed to pass your classes, but you have also been an inspiration for the type of educator I hope to be.

Thank you to my mentor, boss, and friend Pete Dulany. I am thankful for all the opportunities you've shared with me. Each and every day you allow me to be a part of this awesome business and I can't thank you enough for sharing your wisdom and experiences with me.

And of course, thank you to my students for learning and growing beside me. You teach me more than I ever would've imagined and I'm continually thankful for each of you.

- Haley

Thanks to my fellow teachers all over the world who encourage the intellectual, spiritual, and emotional growth of our fellow human beings.

Thanks, Haley, for taking on this project with me and for bringing your energy and enthusiasm to all of the schools we work with. It's truly a joy to work with you and I know our schools feel the same way.

Thanks to Melissa for allowing us to run our first custom Breakout session in your classroom. It was the first of many steps for us on this journey and we're both so grateful for your help.

Finally, thanks to my Breakout tester, Riley, who still gets excited with every clue I give her.

- Pete

INTRODUCTION

We're excited about Breakout boxes. If you're reading this, then you probably are too. You may have even already purchased the materials for a Breakout box, or had a group of students try to work through their first Breakout challenge.

We've seen first-hand how exciting the challenge of Breakout boxes in a classroom can be - whether you're a kindergarten teacher or a high school math teacher. We've introduced the concept of Breakout boxes to schools across the country, and are always excited to see the results. After running over a hundred Breakout sessions over several months, though, we noticed something unusual:

Many teachers are hesitant to make their own Breakout box clues.

These same teachers usually feel comfortable making their own math quizzes, spelling tests, handouts, and interactive whiteboard lessons, but when it comes to a "Breakout box" they tend to rely on the free, pre-made games available in the BreakoutEDU community. While there's certainly nothing wrong with using games others have created, we see lots of comments in the online Breakout community from teachers looking for a particular unit or theme.

If you're one of those teachers, or if you're just getting started with Breakout boxes, then this book is for you. We've created dozens of Breakout games from scratch, a skill we believe is necessary if you want Breakout boxes to become a truly integrated part of your curriculum. While other teachers have great Breakout ideas, we were frustrated by the time it took to fully understand and modify the pre-made scenarios for use in another classroom. We realized that after spending time searching for a Breakout scenario that fits what you teach, going through multiple documents in multiple Google Drive folders, making copies and modifications of the appropriate clues, and then setting the locks and assembling the boxes... well, it took more time (and work) than it would to make one from scratch.

We're not part of the official BreakoutEDU team.

We're technology trainers that have shown the concept of a Breakout box to hundreds of teachers. Over the next few chapters, we'll share our basic process with you for making a custom Breakout activity, give you pointers on what to do and what NOT to do, and even take you through a complete example. By the time you're finished, you'll be ready to create a Breakout box for almost any subject you're teaching.

With a little imagination and creativity, the possibilities of how to include Breakout boxes into your curriculum are endless. After your first personalized Breakout, we think you'll see amazing results - your kids will be cooperating, reviewing, learning, having fun, and asking "When can we do this AGAIN?" So go ahead - invite your students to think outside of the box, make connections, struggle through frustration, succeed through their personal creativity, logic, and critical thinking. We challenge you... to challenge them.

Good luck with your Breakouts!

CHAPTER ONE:
BREAKOUT BASICS

Introducing Breakout boxes into your classroom can provide an innovative, hands-on, interactive, and engaging alternative to traditional classroom activities like worksheets, textbooks, and lectures. Let's face it - while these activities are staples in most classrooms, they can make learning dull and routine after a while. Breakout boxes revolutionize that. It's a fun and interesting way to begin a unit or review a topic.

In addition to being an engaging tool in your teacher toolbox, we love that Breakout boxes push students to discover and practice life skills. Breakout boxes are an excellent way to challenge students to communicate with each other, think critically and creatively, and collaborate effectively. These are skills that are needed in the real world, and Breakout experiences give students a chance to learn and review curriculum and practice those real-world skills at the same time. If you're completely new to Breakout boxes and haven't had a chance to see them in action yet, here's the basic idea:

In a Breakout, students have a wooden or plastic box in front of them that is sealed with multiple locks (See front cover). These locks conceal something inside the box. It could be a small prize, the end of a story, or a congratulatory message. You will give your students a storyline with problems to solve, where they are challenged to "break out" the content of the box. In order to complete the challenge successfully, students will need to follow a series of clues and solve each of them within the given time limit. Each clue is designed to either unlock one of the locks on the Breakout box, or lead the students to another clue. By the end of the challenge, students will have solved all the clues to unlock each of the locks.

 Storytime with Haley:
The Reluctant Learner

"Have you ever had a 'reluctant learner' in your classroom? That one student who just refuses to do most of their work? That one student who is in school because he or she has to be? That one student that just seems to have no motivation whatsoever? We've all seen this at some point, haven't we? As a leader of educational technology trainings, I've come to learn that sometimes there is a teacher in the group who is known to be, well... reluctant to participate in professional development.

Recently, I presented to a new group of teachers that I had never worked with before. One teacher in particular showed her overwhelming excitement as I shared the Breakout box concept to the faculty. She got extremely involved in the session by asking multiple detail-oriented questions and leading every discussion when presented with an opportunity. As teachers filed out of the room when the session ended, a small handful of teachers stuck around to chat with me. After the aforementioned, excited teacher left the room, the other teachers explained that on typical professional development days, this overly-excited teacher usually refuses with all her might to engage in the session. She was described as the 'reluctant learner' of their faculty.

Every time I present Breakout boxes to a group of teachers, I have an eager and interested audience and those reluctant learners tend to suddenly become engaged learners. That was a powerful indication that Breakout boxes really make a difference."

Including Breakout boxes into a curriculum creates an engaging learning environment for all learners, including the 'reluctant learner' mentioned above. These activities engage students because:

- Students have an opportunity to compete against their peers in the classroom.
- Most students are naturally curious about what's inside the box - and the only way they will find out is to break out the contents.
- The concept of a Breakout box is still a relatively new and fresh idea.
- Breakout activities are student-centric. Students are given a chance to talk with their peers and interact with objects. They're not being forced to sit quietly and listen while a teacher speaks.

Teachers love Breakout boxes during faculty meetings for the same reasons. Instead of listening to an administrator talk for an hour, competing against other teachers to break the content out of a box by solving puzzles is much more palatable - especially at the end of a long school day.

We have introduced the concept of Breakout boxes to dozens of schools. Each school is unique in their faculty, grade levels, fluency with technology, physical and technology resources, and financial resources. One of the reasons we firmly believe in the concept of Breakout boxes, and continue to show them to as many schools as we can, is that Breakout boxes can fit ANY content area at ANY grade level. This classroom activity can apply to topics in math, language, science, social studies, music, art, physical education or any other areas of learning. We have seen the Breakout box be successfully integrated into kindergarten classrooms where students compete to "unlock the box" by ripping off pieces of colored tape -- instead of locks that need fine motor skills. We've also seen Breakout boxes integrated successfully at the elementary, middle, and high school levels... even with adult students, parents, and administrative teams. Complexity and difficulty of content and clues can be adjusted to fit the needs of your participants. There is no excuse not to try it!

TAKE ACTION:

Commit to trying a Breakout Box in your classroom as soon as you have the materials for one.

CHAPTER TWO:
PURCHASE OR MAKE YOUR OWN?

There are two schools of thought when it comes to Breakout boxes - you can purchase a pre-made kit from BreakoutEDU, or put together your own kit. There are advantages and disadvantages to each.

We have purchased several kits from BreakoutEDU.com and have recommended that other schools do so. These kits contain special locks, high-quality materials, and guarantees that you will have anything that belongs in a standard kit. It's the easiest way to get the materials for a box, and at the time of this writing, they even work with school purchase orders. The purchase and shipping process can take several weeks, depending on demand, so if you're looking to get started with Breakout boxes right away, it might be better to consider assembling one yourself.

The second option is to assemble your own kit. Most teachers use a combination of materials from Amazon, but supplies can be found at common stores like Wal-mart, Home Depot, Target, and even dollar stores. Anything that can be locked can replace the primary physical box. This could be a lockable toolbox, a hinged plastic storage container, or anything else that locks with a hasp. (We'll talk more about parts later.) The locks themselves can vary according to what you have available to you locally.

Assembling your own Breakout kit does allow you to "customize" the components. For example, if you already have several USB flash drives, or if you are in a 1:1 iPad school with little to no access to things with a USB port, this may not be an item you need to purchase. You may already have various locks that you can use, and as such, the price per kit can go down quickly. With a couple of dollar-store UV pens and a few new locks, some teachers have put together class sets with a combination of new and existing materials for less than $60.

Whether you purchase an official kit or make your own, there are some decisions you need to make before you go shopping. Consider how many boxes your classroom or school may need. We typically like working with four boxes. This gives you four small groups (one group at each box) for a classroom with 16 - 28 students. (Group sizes are 4-7 students.) Obviously, the more boxes you purchase, the smaller groups can be, and there's usually more interaction and participation in small groups. The more boxes you purchase, the more money you'll spend, and the more time it will take to prepare the activities. For upper grade teachers, if you teach the same class several times of the course of a school day, think about your *biggest* class and how many boxes they would need to be successful.

You don't necessarily need four boxes, though. With a little planning and creative manipulation, you can have an entire class of 28 students work together to unlock a single Breakout box. We'll explain how that works a bit later. For now, consider how many Breakout boxes you'll need to create and purchase.

TAKE ACTION:

Consider the needs of your classroom or faculty. Do you want teachers to be able to do Breakout boxes at the same time, on the same day? How many students will be in each group?

While we're focusing on making your own Breakout activities in this book, the folks at Breakout EDU host a variety of pre-made Breakout activities to help get you started. These activities assume that you have a certain set of locks and materials. Become familiar with the following locks, tools, and terms – and if you put together your own kit, you'll want to get the following items from Amazon or a home improvement store:

Breakout box: A large box that is locked and can contain hidden items inside. To complete the challenge, students must unlock the Breakout box. (This is a box we made from wood; cheap plastic toolboxes will do in a pinch.)

Hasp: A clamp placed over the box's lock latch and allows you to add six locks to an area that would typically only fit one.

Three-digit Lock: A standard lock that is opened with any three digit combination. (In earliest versions of the kit, the three digit lock was integrated into the pencil case, which had a three digit lock.)

Four-digit Lock: A standard lock that is opened with four digits in the correct order.

UV Light & Pen: A pen used to write secret messages. UV ink is invisible to the naked eye, but turns blue under ultraviolet light.

Word Lock: A lock that can be opened by putting the letters in the correct order – sometimes to create a word.

Key Lock: A standard lock that needs a key to open. The key may be hidden in a location within the classroom for students to find.

USB Drive: A simple USB drive can be used to store digital clues, links, and files.

Small Lockbox / Pencil Case: A smaller version of the Breakout box that is locked. Usually, the three-digit lock goes here but any lock would work.

Directional Lock: This is a lock that can be opened with a series of moves (up, down, left, right). The length of the combination may vary (up to ten moves with the lock pictured here).

At first glance, it can be difficult to understand how to incorporate some of these locks. The word lock, for example, seems more suitable for an English or language arts classroom rather than a math classroom. The directional lock seems like it naturally fits with an activity on a coordinate plane, but not for a review of a science unit. For now, know that there are ways to make almost ANY clue fit ANY lock, and that we recommend beginners start with at least one of these locks for every Breakout box you're making. The variety of unusual locks contributes to the uniqueness of a Breakout activity.

 Storytime with Pete:
The Sudden Lock Failure

"One day, I was at a school, about to give a Breakout demonstration to a group of K-8 teachers and noticed that the lock on my small pencil case didn't look quite closed. I pushed it in all the way and the lock mechanism just fell apart in my hand. The latch mechanism would shut but any combination - ANYTHING - would open the case. Luckily, the clue that I had assigned for the pencil case was an easy, warm-up clue which the team solved correctly and they opened the case without suspecting anything - but inside, I was sweating bullets the entire time. It made me realize that, just like anything in the world of teaching, you need to have an emergency action plan B."

So, what can you do with last-minute lock failures? There are some things you can do if you discover a bad lock the night before the activity (we'll discuss these later) but otherwise, there's not much you can do. That's why, when purchasing your own materials for a kit (or even if you have a pre-made box) we recommend that you get an extra set of locks, if your budget allows it. That way, if a lock fails, accidentally gets set to a combination you don't know about, or goes missing, you have an emergency backup. This is especially true for directional locks. Many teachers, including us, have had problems with the directional locks. After several sessions, the mechanism occasionally sticks or jams, and sometimes, a perfectly good directional lock will suddenly refuse to open after you've precisely followed the manufacturer's procedure to set the combination to something other than the default factory setting. Even the more costly "digital" version of the directional lock still tends to stick in our experience.

The folks over at BreakoutEDU know this and now have an alternative to the directional lock that seems to be more robust than the traditional directional locks that first came with the kit. They are included in a standard kit if you purchase directly from them, and there are some unique things that you can do with the Breakout locks since the dials are removable.

You'll be happiest if you consider locks ultimately disposable. We need consumable supplies for many things we do in the classroom. Whiteboard markers have a limited life. So do crayons, pens, tissues, batteries, even iPads and Chromebooks... and also things like directional locks. While it certainly is an expense, and as teachers, we fully understand funding challenges, know that you'll eventually need to replace at least one lock in your kit.

Whether you assemble your own Breakout kit or purchase one to save time and be sure you have everything a "standard kit" contains, you're ready to have some fun.

TAKE ACTION:

Based on your budget and what you already have around you in terms of locks, toolboxes, and other materials, determine whether it's best to purchase a complete kit from BreakoutEDU or assemble your own kit.

CHAPTER 3: DIFFERENT BREAKOUTS, DIFFERENT RESULTS

Now that you've assembled or ordered your own Breakout materials, it's time to explore different ways to set up Breakout activities in your classroom based on the resources you may have available. We have seen five common ways of running a Breakout activity, and they all work well. When you create your own Breakout, you'll want to choose the method that best fits your teaching style, personality, resources, and types of clues.

Option One: The Traditional Breakout

The most common way to use a Breakout activity in your classroom is by using Breakout boxes in small groups. In this traditional setting, each small group will have their own Breakout box and clues to work with and manipulate. Each group generally has the same clues, and in the same order, although you can mix up the order of the clues if desired. In most of the schools we work with, teachers end up using this model the most.

Advantages of this option include:

- Each group has their own locks to manipulate and work with, so there's plenty of hands-on experience in each group.
- This format provides a highly competitive atmosphere, which can be energizing for many students.
- Students are responsible for their own box - they can take it around the room or school as they solve clues, if they believe that would be helpful.
- Only a minimal introduction is needed. Put students into groups, set the ground rules, tell the story, and the kids are off and running.
- As a teacher, you can easily float between groups and answer questions as necessary.

Disadvantages of this option include:

- Students may spend more time fiddling with locks instead of solving clues. (This is where good classroom management comes in - walk around the room and ask questions to students that are continually guessing lock combinations.)
- You'll need to purchase approximately four sets of locks and boxes - or enough for small groups to function well in your classroom.
- Extra preparation - every time you want to run a Breakout activity, you'll need to set and create four sets of locks and clues.

We think you'll agree that watching students determine roles within a group and work as a team is very satisfying. As with many classroom activities, the grouping of students for Breakout boxes can greatly impact their success. When creating groups for Breakout boxes, consider differentiation needs, personalities, and learning styles. Whenever possible, we recommend that the teacher group students together who will push each other to succeed. In many groupwork situations, soft-spoken students are overshadowed by other stronger-voiced students. Breakout box activities can give opportunities for these timid students to shine, if the clue happens to be one of their strengths.

If you only have ONE Breakout box for a classroom of 30 kids, have no fear. There are many ways to use a single Breakout box that is still an interactive, collaborative learning experience.

Option Two: The Ticketing System

Another Breakout format to consider is the "Ticketing System." In this format, a single Breakout box will stay in one central location (for example, on your teacher desk) while student groups take turns attempting to unlock a lock on the box. To prepare for a "ticketing" Breakout, you will break your students into groups - just as you would for a traditional Breakout experience. In this system, however, you'll want to classify groups by color, shape, cartoon character, mascot, or some other way to uniquely identify teams. (This is to easily identify which team is turning in a ticket.)

Then, print clues for each team as you would for a normal Breakout experience. In addition, you will give each group an appropriate number of tickets (which can be simple slips of paper that say "Breakout ticket" on them - or something more elaborate that goes with your story / theme, if you prefer). We recommend providing each team with three more tickets than number of locks on the box. For example, if the class Breakout box has four locks, provide each team with seven Breakout tickets. If for some reason, students run out of tickets, you have the option of giving students opportunities to "earn" more tickets through additional practice/challenge problems or other appropriate tasks. These tickets will act as a 1 minute opportunity to try to unlock ONE of the locks. The group turns in a ticket to the teacher, a timer starts, and they can try as many codes as needed during that one minute time frame.

Because only one team can attempt to unlock a lock at a time, students will form a physical line a reasonable distance away from the desk when they are ready to "cash in" a ticket. When each group unlocks a lock, they will take it off, show it to the teacher so he or she may note it, and set the lock to a random starting point such as "000." (This way, when another group attempts to unlock the lock, the students do not see the combination that the previous group tried.) Once every group has opened every lock, the teacher will allow all groups to huddle around the box for the "grand reveal" of the final storyline, mystery prize, or whatever's in the box.

Optionally, the group that is first to properly take off a lock gets additional participation points for the activity or some other reward appropriate for your classroom.

During the activity, you can record when a team has been able to unlock one of the locks by using a table like the one below:

Lock	Team #1 (Blue Team)	Team #2 (Red Team)	Team #3 (Yellow Team)	Team #4 (Green Team)
3 digit lock			X	
4 digit lock	X			
Word lock		X		
Direction lock			X	

This system can work in any class size, with almost unlimited numbers of groups. It takes little preparation on the teacher's part and can lend itself well to almost any Breakout activity. We recommend that you mix up the order of clues within each group when you have multiple groups working on the same box.

Advantages of a "ticketing system" include:

- You can run a Breakout activity for the entire class from a single box, thus saving the expense and setup time for multiple boxes.
- Students spend more time communicating their ideas and developing answers that the whole group agrees upon and less time trying endless combinations to a lock.
- There's generally less wear and tear on the physical locks, which means less replacement of locks, and because the teacher collects the locks as the activity progresses, there's no chance of a student either accidentally or intentionally changing the lock to another combination.

Drawbacks of this system include the wasted time while students wait in line for their turn to unlock the next lock - if necessary, simply lower the time limit for each group to 30 seconds to keep the line moving.

Option Three: Blended Learning / Center Activity

If you only have one set of locks and one Breakout box, students can work together in small groups during a rotation of center activities. This is most appropriate for a blended learning environment or an elementary / middle school classroom which uses centers regularly, but the technique can be adapted for other grade levels.

The basic principle of the Breakout box doesn't change -- students are still working in small groups to try to open the box by solving a series of clues or puzzles.

Advantages of the "center" approach include:

- This adds a new, exciting option to center activities. Many teachers have a math center, a science center, and now a "Breakout" center.
- Teachers only need to purchase a single set of materials, which may be more manageable in a time of ever-decreasing budgets.
- Teachers only need to manage a single Breakout box. There are only a few locks to reset to another combination instead of a dozen or more. You'll still need to create a set of clues for each group of students that will rotate through the centers, or be sure that the clues are set in such a way that they'll stand up to some classroom wear and tear. (For example, some teachers will laminate their clues to give them some longevity. Be sure that if you are laminating a clue with the UV pen, that you do the UV maker first, and THEN laminate the clue. Otherwise, the marker wears off easily.)

There are a few drawbacks to the center-based model:

- Depending on the students and the clues, Breakouts can be rowdy and exciting. Be sure that students understand the expectations you have for their behavior in such a center.
- If students are allowed to talk to students in another group while in another center, they can easily share the clues and answers ahead of time. This is especially true if center activities pause before lunch and resume after recess. Generally, teachers don't have the time to adjust locks and clues in between center rotations. Again, be sure students understand the expectations you have for their behavior. (We've found that students that work on Breakout activities in centers truly don't want to ruin it for other students and are good about keeping the solutions quiet.)
- If you create a Breakout activity as a center, decide whether you or a teacher's aide will be stationed at that center or if you'll be working with another group of kids. If you won't be personally supervising the center, have a classroom procedure to ask for a hint if the group gets "stuck" (or make sure students understand that, in this format, there are no hints available).

Option Four: Part of Exit Tickets

Some teachers use the Breakout box as a small portion of each day of the week. At the end of the daily lesson, students will receive a "daily clue" as part of the exit ticket which summarizes what students have learned. Students talk in groups, compare answers, and explain their thinking. Once students believe they have solved the daily clue, choose one student at a time to come to the front and try the lock. Each day, if they are successful, they will unlock one of the locks as a class. This way, students have something to look forward to at the end of the daily lesson and their exit ticket has a more visible, student-centered purpose. This system builds routine in your lesson, and at the end of the week, students can complete the box and receive the reward or prize on the inside. (We'll talk about rewards and prizes in a later chapter - while these are completely optional, it doesn't have to be anything expensive. It can be something simple like a pencil, homework pass, or a five minute recess extension for the following week.)

With this option, students are generally eager to work on the box each day. They "chip away" at each lock and watch as their hard work culminates in completing the challenge at the end of the week. As the teacher, you only need to set a single box and unlock it over the course of the week, and if students don't solve a clue within the school day, that can be given as a "think about it" homework assignment.

This is definitely a different kind of Breakout experience - students are not as competitive, much more reflective, and time isn't much of a factor. Additionally, as a teacher, you'll feel more compelled to have your students actually get into the box since it spans the course of an entire week. If this happens over and over again, students may realize that they don't need to put a whole lot of effort into solving clues and opening the box, since the teacher gives away enough information on Friday to make sure it's a success.

Still, once the novelty of a Breakout box experience wears off, this is a neat twist on the traditional Breakout experience.

Option Five: Digital Breakouts

Digital Breakout activities have the same elements as normal or traditional Breakout sessions. As the name implies, the only difference is that there are no printed or physical materials for the Breakout experience. In order to participate, students will need to be connected to the Internet using a device such as a laptop, Chromebook, iPad, or desktop computer. The traditional wooden or plastic box is replaced with a Google Site. Each "lock" is represented by an input space on an embedded Google Form. (With data validation, a Google Form can still require clues to be 3 digits, 4 digits, a single word, a series of directions, etc.) Digital Breakouts eliminate the hassle of purchasing and resetting locks, and organizing/printing/sealing/hiding clues.

Critical thinking is taken a step further when challenged by a Digital Breakout because the clues are not numbered and ordered as they are in a traditional Breakout. Instead, students will investigate one simple page filled with hidden links, text, and images to find the clues to solve the

Breakout. In this book, we will not get into digital breakouts in great depth. Creating a digital Breakout activity requires a comfortable understanding of various technologies which we may include in additional releases of this book. Once you get comfortable making your own clues (which is one of the primary goals of this book), you can easily transfer those clues into a Google Form.

As of the time of this writing, BreakoutEDU contains a guide on how to create digital breakouts, and we recommend that you review that guide and determine whether a digital Breakout is appropriate for your classroom.

Advantages of digital Breakout experiences include:

- You don't need to purchase a kit or create your own. Simply get the Breakout EDU password by signing up to be a beta tester. Complete the form on the Breakout EDU webpage at www.breakoutedu.com/beta.
- You have much more leeway with "passwords" for clues. A Breakout "Word Lock" for example, can only spell out certain five-letter words. A Google Form can take everything from a single letter to a 20-word limerick.
- Everything is digital, which eliminates the need to use ink / print on paper, envelopes, and other consumable materials. It also eliminates lock hassles and can be done remotely.

Disadvantages of digital Breakouts include:

- If the school's Internet connection is down or slow, this will greatly impact how your game works out. (Hint: It won't turn out well.)
- Student collaboration can be diminished with a digital Breakout experience, but it might make for an excellent sub plan to make sure students are actively working.
- The lack of physical locks here is detrimental to students that learn better via actual physical touch. There's no satisfying "clink" when a digital lock "unlocks" with the correct code or answer.

Ultimately, it's up to you which style of Breakout boxes you prefer. It's also okay to try one box with a class using the ticketing system and then to use the "traditional four box system" as you get additional materials. Keep it fresh, and create meaningful experiences for your students that you are comfortable with.

TAKE ACTION:

After reading about the various types of Breakout formats, which one speaks to you the most? Which format can you / your school afford? Decide which type of Breakout activity you'd like to try first, once you have all of your Breakout materials.

CHAPTER 4: BREAK OUT OF THE MOLD!
10 STEPS TO MAKING YOUR OWN BREAKOUT BOX

All right, you have your Breakout kit materials and you have some idea as to what a Breakout activity might look like in your classroom. You may have read through some of the pre-made activities on the BreakoutEDU site, or tried to decipher someone else's Google Drive folder with Breakout clues inside. Maybe you were even a participant in someone else's Breakout activity or you tried a pre-made option with your class. If you haven't done any of that yet, RELAX. It's okay. When we made our first Breakout activity for a second grade classroom, we hadn't done any of that either. We spread out all of our materials, found a room with a whiteboard and just started drawing:

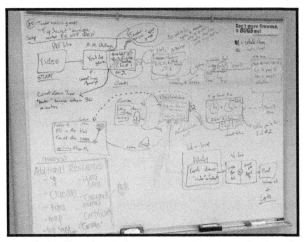
Our first self-made Breakout Activity notes on a whiteboard

In hindsight, we took a simple process and made it more complex than it needed to be. *This was our motivation for creating this guide.*

We decided to do a custom activity because we were having a hard time trying to watch videos, navigate Google Drive folders, and see how we could put an admittedly promising idea into action for second grade. By the time we got finished, we realized that we really ignored most of what was already created in favor of our own clues.

And, overall, our activity was a success. The second grade classroom that we visited LOVED the activity which included a mixture of math, science, and language arts clues that were created specifically FOR THEM.

We highly recommend making your own Breakout box clues for the following reasons:

- You know your kids best - both in what they can handle in an activity like this, and what they actually studied in class.
- You know what technology you have available to you - if you don't have a computer lab and are in a 1:1 iPad school, any premade clue that depends on a USB drive will need to be re-worked.
- Good Breakout experiences have good stories associated with them - and we believe that most teachers are good storytellers. Work the name of your school, principal, or a teacher from your department - heck, even your student names - into the story and the activity suddenly becomes meaningful. Your students firmly believe that this activity was custom-created for THEM, and though they may not always show it, they'll appreciate the work that goes into it.
- While Breakout boxes are certainly fun and engaging things that result in a lot of critical thinking, there are only so many school days in the year. AP courses at the secondary level are often planned out *to the day* at the beginning of the year. There just may not be a good time to take a break for something extra. But, with just a little effort, you can make a Breakout activity that perfectly aligns with your textbook, your handouts, your curriculum. While it may take a little longer, we think you'll agree that the results are worth it.

Before you design your own Breakout activity, we recommend the following:

- If possible, connect with someone who has run or participated in a Breakout experience. You'll get an idea of what it's like from both the participant's and facilitator's perspectives.
- Start small. We finally decided on about six clues, an introductory video, and a celebration at the end. Your first Breakout doesn't need to be any longer than three clues for 20 minutes. It doesn't need to take an hour, nor do you have to use every lock. This gives you practice in making and facilitating the activities, and it gets your students used to opening unfamiliar locks (like the directional lock).

After we designed Breakout activities for several more schools, we realized that if we followed a certain process, the Breakout activity worked well and the time needed to create the Breakout box was significantly reduced. The steps that follow make up the basic process that we go through any time we make a custom box, whether the activity is for 10 people or 100 people. Throughout this section, we'll ask you to stop and "take action" as we go. Scribble your thoughts on a sheet of paper, a Google Doc, or the back of a Starbucks napkin as you go through this section. By the end, you'll have the framework for your own custom Breakout box.

Step One: Set a purpose.

One of the obvious questions that we need to ask as teachers is, "Why are we doing this, anyway?" Is our Breakout box there to provide motivation? A review of what we've already learned? Take a deeper dive into something we read about? All of these are valid answers - but it's a question that needs to be answered regardless of whether you are using a pre-made Breakout activity or one that's your own creation.

Breakout boxes can motivate participants with their high-energy, competitive format. This breaks up the monotony of an otherwise dull activity – for students OR teachers. An after-school meeting listening to a principal talk about new school procedures isn't very appealing after a long day of working with kids. But put us up against our colleagues in a friendly battle of wits? We'll take that almost anytime.

Let's look at the benefits of using a Breakout box as a *pre-teaching* activity, where the students are going in blind, without any knowledge of the subject they're about to encounter.   They're about to use clues to research something and explore a topic that you haven't taught before. For example, let's say you're a junior high social studies teacher about to start a unit on the American Civil War. You want your students to eventually recognize that the Civil War was about more than just "slavery" by using

Breakout clues. The advantages of using this as a pre-teaching activity include:

- The Breakout box provides an interesting twist to a unit introduction -- it's new and different. Rather than announce, "Take out your books and turn to page 75," it's clear from the very beginning that students will become more active learners where they can read, research, discuss, and even learn how to resolve differences of opinion with classmates. This mirrors what we do in the real world, and students will appreciate this authentic learning style.
- All students should start out at about the same ability level because they know very little about the topic. This gives no group an advantage, and making the groups is a bit easier.
- Students will encounter terms and words during the Breakout activity that warrants a discussion later. During the reflection / activity wrap-up, you might hear, "Mr. Z, we saw the word "abolitionist" a few times during the activity and even though we looked it up, I'm still not so sure what that means." This is a great jumping off point into a class discussion or further instruction.

Breakout boxes can also be used as an assessment, either in the middle of the unit or at the end of a term, just before a unit exam. Once you've had a chance to teach a concept, students can complete a Breakout activity to prove to you that they understand it.

Breakout boxes are useful for review because:

- Most students will be at the same level. Unless they've been absent from class (physically or mentally), they'll have a basic knowledge of unit terminology and will be able to make sense of more challenging and complex clues.
- When a group of students actually opens the Breakout box and completes the activity, there is a real sense of accomplishment.
- If students have trouble with a particular clue or section, both the students and teachers will realize this. Students know that they have to study that section more, and teachers can take a few minutes to review it before giving the assessment.

Whether you're using the Breakout activity as a pre-teaching exercise, as a way to further the students' understanding of a concept, or as a review activity, this is a great way to take something that's teacher-centric and make it more student-centric.

TAKE ACTION:

Take a look at what you're teaching over the next few weeks and find a lesson or unit that could use some more student-centric action. Is there something that you've taught in the past that students don't seem excited to learn? That's a great place to start. If you're a secondary teacher, decide which classes, period(s), and units you'll do this with.

If you're an elementary teacher, pick a subject (math, science, etc.) and decide to use a Breakout box with an upcoming lesson. Write down a general use.

For example: "In two weeks, I'm teaching a unit on the American Civil War with my Junior High Social Studies classes. Normally we watch a video or read from the text, but instead, I'll use the Breakout boxes to introduce the factors that led the United States to Civil War."

Step Two: How much time do you have?

Decide how much time you have for the activity. At the upper grade levels, class times are limited to 45 to 55 minutes. This is usually a good length of time for students to work on boxes -- too much time, and the students get tired of the high-intensity, competitive atmosphere a Breakout box normally provides.   Too little time, and students don't have the ability to really think critically and explore the clues.

Some upper grade teachers will let a Breakout activity last for multiple class periods -- each team has the ability to collaborate, think about the problems at home, do further research, and come back to the classroom with ideas in mind. The boxes are simply stored until the next student contact period so that each team can resume their specific box the following day. Keep in mind that if you teach at this level, and have multiple sections of the same class, you'll need to either have enough breakout boxes for every class, (which can become cost-prohibitive for some schools) or stagger the times each section works on the Breakout boxes.

Elementary and middle school teachers can take 30 to 75 minutes to run the activity, or even release clues to students over the course of an entire school day. There is more flexibility here, but Breakout activity lengths should be limited to the appropriate time for your age group. A second grade class may be limited to 30 minutes, while a

6th grade classroom could spend closer to 60 minutes on their boxes.

Regardless of the grade level, we recommend that your first Breakout experience be something relatively simple - this will introduce your students to the nature of the activity and give them practice in basic mechanics of things like opening locks. (Because the locks used with most Breakout boxes are fairly unique, younger students may have a difficult time with operating the combination locks the first time they are used.)

One critical part of the Breakout activity is reflecting on the experience - giving students the ability to openly discuss the clues and their lines of thinking. Be sure that your total time includes at least a few minutes for students to give you feedback. This will help you in planning subsequent Breakout boxes.

TAKE ACTION:

Decide how much time you can dedicate to the activity you wrote about in step one.

Step Three: Decide what specific content will be covered.

The third step in the process is to ask yourself, "What SPECIFIC CONTENT do I want my students to review?" For example, a second grade teacher might have spent the last week teaching students how to recognize and count paper bills and coins. One Breakout clue might include counting play money to get a total sum. That number can be used as the answer to a clue which would open a Breakout lock.

Let's say we put $2.06 in play coins into an envelope, and say nothing else. If students correctly count the money and end up at that number, they can try to put "206" as the combination of a three digit lock or a locked pencil case, which reveals another clue.

After working with money, the second grade teacher spent some time reviewing analog clock times. This is another easy clue - give students an envelope of printed analog clocks and ask the students to find the time that occurs most often. This time could be, say, 11:25, which is the combination to a four digit lock.

For upper grades, break down the basic topic you wrote down in step one. For example, if you are going to create a Breakout box about the American Civil War, what do you want the clues to be about? Perhaps you talked about the Missouri Compromise, the Abolitionist Movement, and the Dred Scott decision - simply assign each subtopic to be a different clue and ask yourself what you'd like the students to learn more about for that clue.

TAKE ACTION:

Decide on at least 3 different types of problems you'd like students to work on over the activity, adjusting this number for the amount of time you decided to spend in step two. Notice that you're not actually creating the clue yet, but rather figuring out more specific topics.

<u>Step Four: What technology do you have that you can use?</u>

Each technology lends itself to different types of clues. For example:

- iPads work well with the BreakoutEDU "Locks" app, QR Codes, Augmented Reality, or anything that has a subject-specific app in the iOS app store.
- Chromebooks can show Flash content, work a little better with Google Docs than an iPad will, and can make use of USB drive clues.

- Computer labs work well for things that require a very precise and specific "click," like a mapping program or software-based problems.
- If you have a 3D printer at your disposal, it can be used to create custom objects that can be measured or otherwise contribute to the activity.

We talk more about different types of clues and how they relate to technology in the following chapter.

TAKE ACTION:

 Write down the technology that you have available to you for this Breakout activity. Will you ask students to use an iPad? Will you be able to reserve the Chromebook cart during the same week another grade is going through standardized testing? Are you going to use any technology at all? Pick technology that works reliably in your classroom. If you know that your room doesn't have a good wireless signal, and that the activity might work better in the computer lab, then keep in mind the use that location and technology for your Breakout lesson.

Step Five: What type of Breakout activity will you run, and what will the groups look like?

We talked about the various ways to run a Breakout experience in chapter three. Decide which format you'd like to use. This will depend on the amount of Breakout boxes you have available to you, and what you're comfortable with. At this point, some teachers will also create a PowerPoint, Keynote, or Google Slides presentation with a list of groups and the students assigned to each. That way, on the day of the Breakout activity, as students enter the room, they know which group they are assigned to, and where they should sit. This gives you maximum class time for the activity and reflection - you're not wasting precious minutes getting ready at the beginning of class.

TAKE ACTION:

Use your favorite presentation tool to create a slide that shows each student and what group they're assigned to. This will be on your classroom projector as students walk in.

Step Six: Create the clues, then match it to a lock.

Use your decisions in previous steps to craft a clue and match it to a lock. This step is so important that we've dedicated the next two chapters to it. It's where most of the work comes in, and it's where having another teacher or person with you to talk out the clues really helps. If you can, find another teacher at your grade level to talk through the clues with you. Keep in mind that the clues must be kept at your grade level. Give your students a reasonable chance of success at breaking out of the box.

We recommend that you read through the next two chapters to fully understand the different types of clues that you can make. Once you have your clues made, the final steps are fairly straightforward.

Step Seven: Decide on a storyline and rewards.

A good story is key to setting the mood for your Breakout box. Give students a *reason* to break the content out of the box and motivate them to complete the Breakout activity. Answer the questions: "Why is there a locked box here?" and "Why do your students need to open it?" By giving students an exciting story, you're also giving them a reason to engage in the activity. This works at all grade levels. The story can be funny, related to the topics of the unit you're studying, take on a pop culture theme (Star Wars is an easy theme, especially if a new movie is about to come out), or otherwise fit into the interests of your students. We've learned that a storyline of "We need to break out before *blank* happens", "when the timer runs out, *blank* happens," or "someone is trying to break out before us because of *blank* evil plan" is an easy way to tell a story.

Next, decide what goes inside the box. What do you want your students to find in there after they've successfully cracked open those locks? Remember, regardless of grade level, students will be curious about what might be inside the Breakout box. Consider what motivates your students. Many teachers include a simple "WE BROKE OUT!" sign which they can then hold up high with pride, as the teacher snaps a quick photo to capture the glorious moment. In some situations, simple prizes like pencils and stickers are appropriate. Other teachers get a little more creative with what they put inside.

To keep students interested and engaged in a Breakout box activity, mix up what rewards are inside of the physical box. Rewards don't have to be tangible objects. Simple things like homework passes, extra recess, or free time tend to be valued rewards by elementary, middle, and high school students.

On occasion, we have replaced the physical reward or treat inside the box with a fun final activity instead. If you're thinking about including an ending activity instead of a reward, think about a "one minute challenge" (there's a popular game show that's full of these kinds of challenges) like stacking plastic cups, making play dough creations, pinning the tail on the donkey... even flinging ping-pong balls at the enemy of the storyline.

Some teachers debate whether or not there should actually be a reward or prize in the box. They argue that students should celebrate the problem solving, communication success, and what it takes to complete a Breakout activity rather than the little value of the prizes inside so that students do not become unmotivated or disappointed with repetitive prizes.

Should you reward your students with chocolate, pencils, or stickers, or should you celebrate the completion of the box? We've found that in many cases, the journey of the Breakout, the excitement, and the competition is far more valuable than the physical reward inside the box... but we'll also usually put some kind of small reward in the box. As with everything else, this is entirely up to you.

TAKE ACTION:

What story are you going to tell, and what reward can you put inside the Breakout box that is approved by your administration, with little cost, and your students will actually want?

Step Eight: Print the clues and set the locks

This step is pretty easy - it's where you give the clues you created in step six another pass through spell-check and set the locks. To set the locks, follow the manufacturer's instructions EXACTLY. Most of the time, this means opening the lock, using a small screwdriver or pen tip to move something into the "reset" position, setting the new combination, and then moving out of the "reset" position again.

We've learned that in most Breakout sessions, clues should be given in a specific order and in some cases, even build on one another. We recommend creating envelopes for each clue and labeling them "Clue #1", "Clue #2", and so on. While many teachers like to hide clues around the room to get kids moving, we typically like taping these envelopes to the physical breakout box so that once groups are finished with the first clue, they can immediately move on to the second, without needing teacher assistance. Before beginning the Breakout, be clear in your instructions that teams should only be working on one clue at a time.

(Of course, if you'd rather have your students working on clues simultaneously, instead of sequentially, you can... but we've found that this can lead to decreased teamwork and collaboration.)

Step Nine: Practice / Get ready

Verify that your locks actually open once you've set them. Once you have, fill the boxes with the final storyline, prizes and reflection cards if you're using them, then add the hasp and all of the locks. As you add locks to the hasp, be sure that you're putting the locks on in such a way where it's easy to read the letters, squeeze the directional lock, etc. Putting the locks on backwards will frustrate and slow a group down enough to the point where it gives other groups a competitive advantage.

At this point, you can also put the boxes in the room, put any clues in their proper positions, and get your timer ready for action. When we need a quick, full-screen countdown timer, we like to use e.ggtimer.com but this does require Internet access. Any other countdown timer you may have in your teacher toolbox works just fine here.

Step Ten: Prepare for reflections and adaptations

Decide how you'd like the class to reflect on the Breakout experience. If you will ask students to fill out a Google form as an exit ticket, have the link ready. If you're having a class discussion at the conclusion of the activity, write down three or four good "conversation starter" questions. Some of our favorites include questions like:

- What was the most challenging clue to figure out, and why? What made the clue difficult?
- How did your team work together to solve a clue?
- What would you have done differently if you had to do it over again?
- How did your team resolve differences of opinion?
- Tell me about a great success or an "Ah-ha!" moment.

Take an answer from each group and have them share with the class.

So those are our ten steps to creating a custom Breakout. Let's dig deeper into the crafting of specific, detailed clues.

CHAPTER 5:
WHAT TYPES OF CLUES CAN I MAKE?

In this chapter, we'll talk about our favorite types of clues to include in a Breakout box. While there are many clues besides the ones discussed below, these are our favorites.

Here's the "quick list" of clues we used when first getting started and continue to use regularly in a Breakout box:

- Crossword Puzzles
- Google Forms
- Re-ordering text clues
- QR codes
- Mini-worksheets
- Puzzles, Codes and Ciphers
- Clues with manipulatives
- Red Herrings

Let's talk about each one, why we like to use it, which technologies you'll need (if any), and how it matches up with locks.

Crossword Puzzles

Crosswordlabs.com is a free online printable crossword generator to use as a clue. (They also work well for hint cards, or in combination with other problems.) These crossword puzzles work best to open the WORD lock because you can ask students to review vocabulary, look up definitions, and there are letters everywhere in the clue. Simply circle blank spaces in the crossword puzzle with a red pen (for easier clues) or the invisible UV pen (for harder clues) to make students re-order those magic circles to spell something with the word lock.

Another crossword puzzle maker we've been using for years is Eclipse Crossword - these folks have a downloadable, installable program for PC only (sorry, Mac folks) but it's easy to use to create and save crossword puzzles. It's free, and can generate either electronic puzzles (which you could self-host on a blog somewhere) or printable puzzles.

Google Forms

One of the most versatile and helpful tools to create your own Breakout Box is a Google Form. Google Forms are easy to use, modify, copy, and share with others.

Let's explore some of the advantages of incorporating Google Forms into your Breakout clues.

Data Validation

Google Forms are especially helpful in creating math problems. Let's assume that you give a math problem to a student to solve, and she gets 42.3. *Your* calculations came out to an answer of 42.5. Both you and your student have done the correct mathematics; you've just rounded to different precisions. As a result, if you were to create a combination lock with "425" and the students kept entering "423", there'd be a lot of wasted time on the student trying to figure out rounding. (It's best to try to avoid this altogether by providing detailed instructions.)

This is where Google forms becomes helpful. By creating a one-question, short answer form, we can provide for this little margin of error.

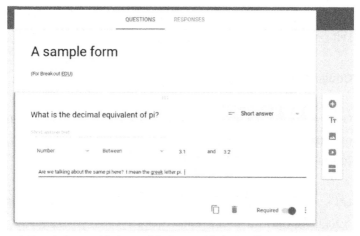

A Google Form with data validation enabled – it will accept any value between 3.1 and 3.2

In this example, if the student puts in any value between 3.1 and 3.2 (like 3.14 or 3.141), he or she will be taken to the form's confirmation page. Any other value, and the student will see our feedback. ("Are we talking about the same pi here?")

Matching Forms to Locks

One of the great things about Google Forms is that you can use it with any lock. Your confirmation page (which students will only see once they put in the correct value) can tell students to:

- Enter LASER (on a word lock)
- Enter 3-4-4-1 (on a combination lock)
- Enter UP-DOWN-LEFT (on the directional lock - Be sure to specify all CAPS and with dash marks and no spaces)
- Find a key in another location (taped to the bottom of a desk or object)
- Go to another physical location for the next clue (the cafeteria, playground, etc.)
- Click on a complicated web link (which they won't have to enter since it's already electronic)

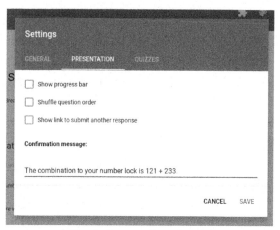

A Google Form confirmation page

Using Web Shorteners

Getting students to a Google Form is pretty easy -- use Google's Web Shortener service at http://goo.gl and paste in the long Google Form preview URL (which always ends in "viewform"). It will give you a shorter, more typeable version of the Google Form. (Be careful, the links are still case sensitive.)

For example, clicking "View" on a Google Form brings up the following web address, which is too long for students to type correctly.

https://docs.google.com/forms/d/e/1FAIpQLSfsDoFXKpn9Q
bAxCfSMTA6UID0gGnULgLa7SiS6GmWIuRoMOg/viewform

Using the goo.gl web shortener, this becomes much easier to type: goo.gl/QGu5ST

The goo.gl Google Web Shortener

The other nice thing about a Google Form is that it can be updated after you've created it and printed the clue. Sometimes I'll create a Google Web Shortener Link, print it, and seal it in a mysterious "envelope #1" and then later that night, wish I had provided more or less clarification, adjust the difficulty, or provide additional instructions. I can go back and change the Google Form without having to re-print anything or waste additional envelopes. When my students complete the activity, they'll see only the updated form.

Drawbacks

One drawback to Google Forms that we've found -- and we've never had a group of K-8 or teachers figure this out until we've said something -- is that anyone can right-click on a Google Forms page and, with a little detective work, figure out what value you need to enter to move on. A crafty middle school or high school student may figure this out, but you're safe otherwise. (If your students have iPads, and not Chromebooks, this is much harder to do. Viewing the source of a webpage isn't a standard option on the Safari or Chrome iPad browser at the time of this writing.)

Further, you may need to adjust the security settings of your Google Form, depending on your school's Google settings. If you will allow students (or other teachers) to use their cell phones or other personal devices to access the clues, be sure that your form's security settings are correct - you want to be sure that "Must be a member of schooldistrict.org" is UNCHECKED on the form settings. This way, if they're signed in to a normal Gmail account, or don't have a Google account at all, accessing the form is no problem.

The possibilities with Google Forms are endless. For this reason, we usually leave a Google Form until after we've made clues for other locks. Whatever is left can almost always match up with a Google Form.

Reordering text clues

Anything that can be re-ordered makes for a great Breakout box clue. This could be important lines from Hamlet, elements of the periodic table, solving a math problem and then putting the numbers in some kind of order, etc. This works with almost any kind of lock and it's low-tech.

For example, the following quotes / lines come from Shakespeare's Hamlet.

F *"That it should come to this!"*
C *"This above all: to thine own self be true."*
A *"Though this be madness, yet there is method in't."*
E *"To be, or not to be: that is the question."*
D *"The lady doth protest too much, methinks."*

To use these quotes as a Breakout Clue, simply print them out, cut the lines apart, and place them into an envelope. The correct sequence is F-C-A-E-D, which a Word lock can be easily set to. (If you've already used a Word lock and need this to be a directional lock clue, just replace the letters in front of the quotes with arrows: ← → etc. and set the lock appropriately.

QR Codes

QR Codes are a quick and easy way to get students to a website or a research page to look for a clue. We recommend using qrstuff.com and qrcode.kaywa.com to create printable QR codes. If you are a Chromebook school and want to incorporate QR codes in your Breakout, consider using THE QR Code extension on the Chrome Web Store to scan QR codes via the Google Chrome web browser.

If you need a simple QR Code that works - even without Internet access, set the QR Code type from URL to "Text." When creating a textual QR code, you have a limited number of characters to work with, but it's enough to give a good Breakout clue.

If you'd like your Breakout to continue on the playground, school athletic field, or another place in the school that might have spotty Internet access, we highly recommend the "text" version of this clue.

Mini Worksheets

While Breakouts can help to replace a boring, ho-hum worksheet, you can always take a full or half worksheet and make that a quick, easy clue. For example, K5Learning.com and many other sites online offer a wide variety of practice worksheets for free. If you're trying to use the Breakout box as a review, find one of these handy worksheets and pull a few problems from it. Math worksheets work exceptionally well for 3 and 4 digit locks. Worksheets can be difficult (like graphing functions) or easy (two digit number addition). Ask your students to count the number of ODD answers on a worksheet and add 1200, and you've got an easy combination to a 4 digit lock! Worksheets from your class textbook or curriculum company work too.

Puzzles, Codes, and Ciphers

There are unlimited amounts of decoders and cipher tools available online. Ciphers, codes, and puzzles add an extra level of complexity to your Breakout box clues at any grade level. Students are forced to use critical thinking skills to expand upon the original meaning of the clue. Students will need to recall or locate information, and dig deeper to develop strategies of solving more complex problems.

We suggest beginning with a puzzle, especially at younger grade levels. (When we use the term puzzle, we mean that students simply need to connect pieces together to determine the hidden meaning behind the clue.) This can be done with physical hand-cut puzzle pieces or created online by using a site like jigsawplanet.com. (We suggest this website because it works well on both iPads and Chromebooks / computers.)

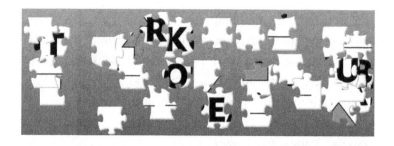

An example puzzle created with Jigsaw Planet, before and after assembly

The image above is an example of one of four jigsaw puzzles the students would have to put together to solve this clue completely. This image reveals the first direction (UP) in the sequence of four directions. Each puzzle would reveal the next direction in the directional lock's combination.

To challenge and elevate a student's logical and creative thinking, try including an activity where students have a code and use a given codebook to figure out the meaning. The decoder table below can be used to transfer words into directions used to open the directional lock. The word "HOUSE" translates to the code: "Left, Up, Right, Up, Up."

Decoder Table

A	↑	N	←
B	↓	O	↑
C	→	P	↓
D	←	Q	→
E	↑	R	←
F	→	S	↑
G	↓	T	←
H	→	U	→
I	←	V	↓
J	↑	W	→
K	→	X	←
L	↓	Y	←
M	→	Z	↓
0	←	5	↓
1	↑	6	→
2	→	7	←
3	↓	8	←
4	→	9	↓

A quick decoder table allows you to convert letters and numbers into the directions left, right, up, or down.

Solutions to clues can be manipulated to fit the locks you already have by using decoders. Therefore, if you have three clues that end up being numerical answers, it is not necessary to purchase additional number locks that aren't included in your original set. Similarly, if you've created two clues that need to have word answers (Let's say…. SPY and LASER) you do NOT need to go out and by another word lock. Instead, try using a decoder like this one. Have students use the word "SPY" and translate it using the image below:

An easy translation between letters and numbers

The solution SPY can become the code 779. Now instead of purchasing an additional word lock, you can use your three digit lock for this solution.

To challenge students to use critical thinking skills, have them try to solve a clue using a cipher. A group of symbols in a specific pattern are used to depict letters and when strung together, can be "encrypted" as a message. (Think of Morse code which operates this way using dots and dashes.) One of our favorite ciphers to include in our Breakouts is called the "Pig Pen Cipher."

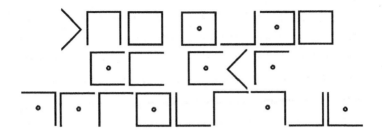

Practice decoding this message as a student would. Take a minute or two to try decoding the message above by using the key below:

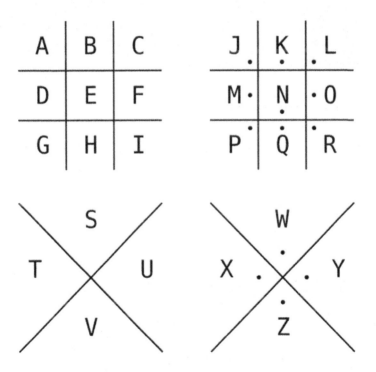

Were you able to figure it out? If you've never used this cipher before, odds are that it took you a minute or two to break this cipher... and that's fine! Codes and ciphers require students to dig deeper with critical thinking to solve a problem, instead of solving it at surface level. This critical thinking is what we believe Breakouts should be all about. (Ready to check your work? ... The above "coded message" says "THE NAME OF OUR PRINCIPAL".)

Using puzzles, codes, and ciphers in your Breakouts provide another level of fun, intrigue, and critical thinking. Best of all, you don't really need technology for this one... it's a very easy, low-tech clue.

Clues with Manipulatives

To add a tactile experience to a Breakout, add manipulatives. For example, print up some fake money and put it into an envelope with a clue. Give students directions to count money, subtract from it, or add it together to solve a riddle or problem.

Storytime with Pete:
A use for 3D printing

"One of my favorite Breakout experiences was with a group of math teachers at a high school. I 3D printed some objects from Tinkercad, a free online design

website, and asked the math teachers to find the surface area and volume of each, which opened the numeric locks.

While you don't need a 3D printer to include manipulatives in a Breakout box, being able to create custom objects – like a hexagonal prism with a missing cylinder in the middle – provides a chance to practice real-world math skills.

Red Herring Clues

When creating Breakout boxes, we occasionally like to be sneaky with our clues and hints. Once a class has been through their first Breakout, we like to add "Red Herring" Clues. These clues mislead or distract students from the main hint and towards a false conclusion. As you can imagine, some students are better at picking up on these distractions than others.

For example, add new posters, arrows, or additional distracting elements to the classroom decor. Students will notice these changes to the classroom environment and assume that these changes are correlated to the Breakout box activity. In reality, they may or may not. Keep your students on their toes. During a subsequent Breakout, make sure they need to use a poster around the room to help solve a clue.

If you and your class are not yet ready for red herring clues, try mixing and matching clues and their ciphers. For example, slip a cipher needed to solve Clue #3 into Clue #2's envelope. Students may wonder why the cipher is needed, but not when. By the time they get to Clue 3 or 4, they may forget about the "extra" thing they had in a previous clue. Similarly, if you're giving students a clue that requires the UV light, try giving them the light in an earlier clue.

All right, you've got some ideas for Breakout clues. These are not our only ideas for clues, but rather the ones that we can consistently go back to over and over again because we know they work well. With a few minor modifications, these clues can work for social studies, science, mathematics, or any other subject.

Let's take a quick look at some further tips, tricks, and pitfalls.

CHAPTER 6: TIPS, TRICKS, AND PITFALLS

By this point, you should have a general idea of what you can do with a Breakout box, and what types of clues you can make. We want your first Breakout boxes to be a success in the classroom. If you're still new to the world of Breakout boxes, here are 15 tips for your first activities. (It's worth mentioning that, as Breakout veterans with hundreds of Breakout experiences, we still like to review this list before going "live" with a new Breakout activity.)

Tip #1: Limit your first box to three clues. It won't take the whole period, and it doesn't have to. Your students will get experience working as a team, practice opening new and unfamiliar locks, and get a feel for what a Breakout is like. By the end of the day, they'll be ready for a tougher and more time-consuming Breakout challenge.

Tip #2: Explicitly state which lock your students are trying to solve within your clue. This helps students to stay on track and move through the puzzles with less confusion, especially at a young grade level. During subsequent Breakouts, once students are familiar and comfortable with the locks, do not tell students which clue corresponds with which lock. Instead, watch as students determine the solution to the clue, and how to apply it to the remaining locks on the Breakout box.

Tip #3: Give students a place to write out a blank solution. For example, for a four digit lock clue, give students four blanks to write out the correct answer before going to the lock directly. At the end of your clue, use the underscore key to make blank spaces. For example:

The Mayflower landed in North America in the year

___ ___ ___ ___.

Tip #4: Keep extra manipulatives to a minimum. Only add necessary objects at first - use basic clues, the box itself, and the locks. Once you've got the hang of Breakout boxes, you can experiment with things like hollowed-out books, STEM circuit kits, 3D printed objects, and other additional materials. Remember that, if you submit a brilliant custom scenario to the Breakout community, other teachers will also need these same "extras."

Tip #5: Re-order clues for each group if you plan on having students working at the same time in close proximity to each other, so that students do not easily overhear other groups working. Students could easily hear a four digit number like "1492" and decide to try that on the four-digit lock without actually solving the clue or puzzle.

Tip #6: Practice your activity at school ahead of time. A school's Internet connection is protected by a firewall, which may prohibit certain websites or content that you plan on using as a clue. If you usually create your lessons at home, we suggest practicing your Breakout box activity AT SCHOOL before running your activity with students. If there are any kind of firewall issues, they should show up during your practice run and you can work with your technology support team or alter the clue to something that the firewall allows.

Tip #7: Do not use long links that students will need to type out correctly to access content. When you are using links, use QR codes and/or URL shorteners. We suggest using bit.ly, goo.gl, or tinyurl.com.

Tip #8: For young students, such as PreK or Kindergarten, use colored tape instead of the difficult locks. Associate each clue with a different colored piece of tape. Once students have solved the clue, have students remove the appropriate piece of tape. If you do not have colored tape available, you may also number blue painter's tape.

Tip #9: Use Google Slides to create printed clues instead of Google Docs. This allows you to add and layer images and text with ease while still retaining the option to collaborate with others. Google Slides will allow you to change the page size to fit a standard piece of printable paper. To do so (as of February, 2017), there are three steps:

Step 1: From your Google account, go to your Google Drive and create a new Google Slide.

Step 2: Select "File", "Page Setup…"

Step 3: Select "Custom", and enter "8.5" and "11" Inches to match a standard piece of printer paper.

After you set the page size, apply a theme if desired, and begin creating clues.

Tip #10: Include a diagram of how to reset the lock when using the directional lock for the first time. Introduce how to use the lock and show students that they will need to squeeze the lock twice in order to be able to clear the lock and try another solution.

Direction 1: North (Up)
Direction 2: _____
Direction 3: _____
Direction 4: _____
Direction 5: _____
Direction 6: _____

** Hint: Did you make a mistake? Squeeze the top of the lock twice and release to "clear" the lock.

Tip #11: Allow students to struggle a bit. If you're running your Breakout and students come across a more complex clue where they need to try multiple lock combinations before coming to the right solution, don't stress. Such struggle supports a growth mindset. Students may fall short the first time, but have additional opportunities within the given time limit to succeed. In the end, students are proud of their authentic success when they unlock each lock from the box.

If you notice a group struggling for several minutes, make sure your students know that it's okay to use hints, and that you'd rather have them ask for help than sit in frustration for extended periods of time. Don't give the clue away during the hint. Instead, ask thought-provoking questions that will give students a chance to successfully open the lock or complete the clue. You may want to do this ahead of time -- try to anticipate which clues your students will have problems with, and what you'll do if they ask you for a clue.

Tip #12: The time it takes to finish one Breakout box will be different from others. This may vary depending on difficulty and the purpose of the Breakout. For example, if a Breakout is being used to introduce an idea or unit, it will take students longer to work their way through it. Alternatively, if the box is being used as a review of material that's already been thoroughly covered, students may work at a quicker pace. Regardless of purpose, practicing your Breakout box at "student speed" will help you figure out the challenge of your Breakout time limit. If you have no idea where to start with time, figure five minutes per clue.

Tip #13: If you can, watch students progress through the clues and get everyone involved by handing clues to students who are sitting back and taking a "back seat" role. We all have students who won't do work if they don't have to (though this typically doesn't happen with a Breakout until late middle school / high school). This can also be included in your ground rules before beginning the activity -- there should not be one student who reads and completes every clue.

Tip #14: Use clues that require critical thinking rather than answers that take a simple search on Google. Clues should push students to think in creative ways.

For example, an art teacher may want to have students associate famous paintings with their artists. Instead of asking students, "Who painted the Mona Lisa?", tell students that they were BORN to succeed at solving a clue with four different pictures of paintings on them, each from a different artist. Students could then add the year that each artist was born and come up with a four-digit number. (Of course, this would open a four-digit lock.)

As an example, see goo.gl/QGu5ST

Tip #15: Reflection is NOT optional. It's a meaningful conclusion to the Breakout activity. Ask questions that require your students to think about their participation, strategies, and the difficulties their team faced. Have your students make suggestions to continually improve the Breakout experiences in your classroom.

 Storytime with Pete:
The Internet's Down!

"One day, I brought our standard set of four Breakout boxes to one of the rural school districts in Illinois that we work with regularly. On this particular day, we tried a new Breakout activity that dealt with digital

citizenship. In order to solve many of the clues, the Breakout participants had to watch a video, answer Google Form questions, and finish an online jigsaw puzzle. About two minutes after we got started, the Internet connection went down and I had to go into "Emergency survival mode." I tried hooking one Chromebook device from each group to my cell phone's hotspot so that everyone would have some kind of connection. It was slow, and it took a long time for things to load (my signal this far out in rural Illinois was weak) but it eventually worked. At that point, I realized the importance of having an emergency backup plan, and to make sure the activity doesn't exclusively rely on an Internet connection."

So, what can you do if the Internet connection goes down?

First, plan your Breakout activity with a mixture of online and offline clues. For example, QR codes can be programmed to display text on a QR scanner without an Internet connection. Include clues with at least some physical manipulatives like printed strips of paper for groups to re-order, which requires no connectivity. If you're working with Chromebooks or in a computer lab, having a clue on a USB Drive (which again, shouldn't require online access) would also work well.

Second, take things offline whenever possible. For example, if you're including a video in the breakout activity for clue #1, have a local copy of the video on your laptop or

Chromebook. (We recommend keepvid.com or a similar site for downloading videos offline.) If the Internet connection goes out, you can pause the timer, call the class together, play the video for all to see on the class projector, and move on.

If your Internet or WIFI connection goes out, and the clue can't easily be converted to something that's accessible offline, then simply remove the clue from the Breakout and make the adjustment consistent with your theme. For example, if a second grade class has a "Perry the Platypus" theme, you can call the class to order and say, "SPECIAL ALERT! Phineas and Ferb realized the Internet was down, so they went five minutes into the future and brought back a clue. The secret to the number lock is 550." You've taken away one of the online puzzles, but you saved the activity from having to be stopped altogether.

As a teacher, we know you're used to thinking on your feet - and Breakout boxes are no exception. If you have a stable Internet connection at school with good speed, and it rarely gives you problems, feel free to depend a little more on the online clues. If it's rare for a week to go by without some kind of Internet connection problem, use common sense and make your clues more "offline" and printed or physical.

CHAPTER 7: AN EXAMPLE BREAKOUT ACTIVITY MADE FROM SCRATCH

 Why are we making custom clues, again? Doesn't that take up a lot of time?

Creating custom clues does take some time, but once you get the hang of it, you won't waste hours sifting through someone else's Breakout clues and trying to figure out how to make it fit into what you're teaching. After creating a few Breakouts of your own, you'll be a pro at creating clues!

Let's assume that you've just taught a 5th grade social studies unit on Westward Expansion. You followed the textbook's explanation - which was good, but not very engaging or relevant to modern-day life. You want to up the "engagement factor" to conclude this unit, and you'd like students to "dig deeper" into the material that you covered together in class. We could go looking online and searching through Google for pre-made clues, but in this case, we want a custom set of clues to match what we actually covered in class, since "Westward Expansion" could encompass so many different things. The odds of someone creating a "Westward Expansion" box that perfectly fits our fifth grade classroom is low, so this is a perfect opportunity for a custom Breakout.

Let's follow our step-by-step method for creating a custom Breakout Box.

Step One: Set a purpose.

We know that we're going to focus on Westward Expansion, and that we're going to ask students to dig a little deeper into some of the topics already covered in class. After the Breakout day is complete, the class can talk about the clues and topics in a whole-group discussion before wrapping up the unit.

Step Two: How much time do you have?

Assume that we'd like this activity to take one class period of about 45 minutes.

Step Three: What *specific content* will be covered?

In this unit, assume the textbook talked about things that happened in the United States between 1800 and 1900, like the importance of the invention of the telegraph, the Louisiana purchase, the Homestead Act (which provided 'free' land to people willing to move west), Native Americans being moved to reserves, the gold rush, and the transcontinental railroad. Ideally, clues from these topics should make their way into the activity.

Step Four: What technology do you have?

Assume that we have an iPad or Chromebook for every group working on this activity, or that we're in the computer lab. None of these activities will be device-specific.

Step Five: What type of Breakout activity will you run, and what will the groups look like?

This will be a traditional Breakout. Assume that we have 20 students and have four boxes available, so each group of 5 students will have a box.

These first five steps should only take a few minutes but they are important to think about because they really set the ground rules for what we're about to do. Now we're ready to make the clues.

Step Six: Create the clues, then match it to a lock.

Here's where the fun (and real work) begins. Follow along as we explore our specific content and use that to generate clues.

Let's start with the telegraph topic from step three. Assume that we talked about the importance of the telegraph in class, and how it rendered the Pony Express useless because a message could be sent over incredibly long distances almost instantly. The textbook talks about the whole notion of "Morse code" which we briefly went over, but I'd like my students to have some practice with actually decoding a message.

A quick search on Google reveals a free and awesome Morse Code Translator that will convert typed text into the short and long "beeps" of Morse code. You can put text into a box, hit "translate" or "play" and it gives an audible, Morse code representation of that text! Awesome! As a bonus, you can download the sound of the Morse code as an MP3 file (great for slow or unreliable Internet connections). The translator is here:

http://morsecode.scphillips.com/translator.html

So, what could we put in there for students to decode? It can't be anything too difficult like a link to a website. (This is likely their first experience with Morse code, and even if you considerably slow the dashes and dots, it can be tricky to decode. Try it!) A short sequence of letters and numbers should work and be doable for fifth grade, so we're going to put in "**Code 124**" which will allow students to open the small box included in a standard Breakout kit. You could also simply attach the three digit lock to the hasp of the main Breakout box.

How do students get to listen to that clue? We can do this a couple of different ways. The easiest way to get students to listen is to hook my teacher computer up to the classroom speakers and play the sound for EVERYONE - so this can be something that the whole class STARTS with. Just play the sound over and over again on repeat until everyone's moved on to the second clue. Great! We just found our clue #1, and don't even need to print anything.

As an adaptation, if the thought of playing Morse code over and over on a class set of speakers frightens you, simply upload the MP3 file to a Google Drive and set the sharing permissions so that "Anyone with the link can view" and students can listen, re-wind, pause, etc. on their own devices.

If I know or think my students won't have Internet access over the course of the day, I would find a "Morse code translation table" from Google and print off a few copies. This could also be used as a "Hint" in case one of the groups really doesn't understand what to do with the sound, or if they're having problems decoding the sound. I could also print out the sound for younger learners. Code 124 becomes:

-.-. --- -... . / .---- ..--- ....-

Second Clue

All right, on to the next clue. Assume that we want students to talk about the end of westward expansion because there was actually a defined point in time when there was no more "frontier" to the old west. It had been explored and settled, and the United States was no longer going to track people moving in and out of that region. (This actually happened in 1890.) A quick Google search on this reveals that most websites simply write that the government had announced an end to the frontier in this year. At this point, we can make our next clue, and it depends on how difficult we want it to be.

If we want this to be an easy clue, we can write something like, "The western frontier was officially declared closed in this year" and set the four digit lock to 1890.

If we want this to be a more difficult clue, we can write something for clue #2 like, "What was the name of the man that officially announced that westward expansion had ended?" This means students need to search for something like "Westward expansion ends" which results in several articles and websites indicating:

- The superintendent of the United States Census in 1890 declared Westward expansion over. (They will in turn search, "Who was the superintendent of the census in 1890?")

- The Superintendent of the Census in 1890 was Robert Porter. This can be found in a citation of a primary source in a Wikipedia article, which attributes the ending of Westward Expansion in 1890 to something written by Robert Porter.

During this clue, students are reading more about westward expansion, questioning sources, and looking at historical things as they go. They're also seeing "1890" over and over again which should cement their knowledge that the western frontier was settled by this point. "Robert Porter" can therefore be the answer to a clue, and we can make this clue unlock something on a Breakout Box in a number of ways.

- The last name "PORTER" can be applied to our standard "directional decoder key" (see our resources section) to translate this into a sequence of six directions to open the directional lock.
- The last name "PORTER" could also be used in a Google Form that requires students to enter the correct answer before seeing the combination to the 4 digit lock, which might be 1893 (The year Porter retired).
- Looking at the WORD lock, we can see that we have 5 letters that almost fit the name. The lock could be set to PORER and the clue could say something like "Take out the T before you TRY."

We could pick one of these options right now, or continue making clues and see which lock we don't end up using.

Because the directional lock can be tricky to incorporate, let's assume that this clue opens the directional lock, set to Down-Up-Left-Left-Up-Left. (PORTER)

Third Clue

For the third clue, let's go back to the Homestead Act. This act allowed people to buy land at a very cheap price as long as the purchaser would agree to improve the property and live there for a while. Specifically, anyone of age that was a citizen of the United States (or intending to become a citizen) could apply for up to 160 acres at $1.25 an acre. This results in a cost of $200 total. There was also a small registration fee of $18 to apply. It takes some work to find the $18 figure and a simple multiplication problem gives the $200 figure, so $218 seems like a good answer to the next clue. As before, we can take the 218 and assign it into a Google Form, the directional lock, or come up with another way to have it open the word lock.

Because Google Forms allow you to specify a range of numerical values, let's use the Google Form for this clue. Some sites mention that $12 was all that was initially needed to file, and so both $212 and $218 could be acceptable answers to this clue. A Google form would allow us to specify a range of anything from $211 to $219 as a correct answer, and that would allow them to open the Word Lock, four digit lock, directional lock, etc. Let's assume that this will open the four-digit lock. On the

Google Form confirmation page, I'll indicate that the lock is set to 9397 (a random combination).

Because we only have 45 minutes for this Breakout (as specified in step two), one more clue should be enough for this activity. Four clues, each at 10 minutes (there's a fair amount of research to most of these clues) equals 40 minutes, and we'll throw in five minutes of "reflection time.")

Fourth Clue

For the fourth lock clue, let's focus on the Transcontinental Railroad. Imagine the textbook talking about the benefits and effects of the railroad, but not the towns it went through. Because students don't necessarily feel "connected" to the railroad, I would like students to see an actual primary source document on the original Transcontinental Railroad.

A quick look at the Wikipedia page on the Transcontinental Railroad page gives shows an original railroad schedule with times and cities. Notice that the very last stop is a place called "Promontory" and that after May 17, 1869, a train that leaves Sacramento at 6:39am will arrive in Promontory at 11:05pm. It doesn't explicitly say *where* that city is. After finding the city in Google Maps (or another favorite resource, Scribble Maps), one can see that it's a city in Utah, which is where the Transcontinental Railroad came to an end. The city of Promontory has a large lake next to it, and that can be used for the final clue.

We haven't used the WORD lock yet, and from past experience (or the sample word list included with the lock) know that one of the words that can be made with it is "WATER." We could have this lock set to WATER and the clue might say something like, "All aboard the Transcontinental Railroad at exactly 6:39am from Sacramento, California! Get off the train at exactly 11:05pm that same day, and go 24 kilometers straight west. Where are you?" Looking at a map -- this IS social studies, after all -- shows that students would be in the middle of the WATER.

At this point we have used four locks: the three digit lock (#1), the directional lock (#2), the four digit lock (#3) and the word lock (#4) which is enough to get students into the box. At this point, we could finish and call it a day, but rather than just have a quick sign that says "We broke out!" we could have a fun, final activity and clue in there.

Final activity

For this final activity, we can use the Gold Rush as a topic. Perhaps we want the students to "dig for gold" once they get inside. To demonstrate that gold mining "required good luck as much as skill and hard work" (See the history.com link in the resources section) we'd like to have a LOT of things for them to dig through, and only ONE of those things allows them a successful completion of the activity.

One component that we haven't used yet which is included in standard kits is the UV light. This allows an invisible message to be written somewhere and seen only with a working UV flashlight. Imagine students getting the last lock off the box, with excitement building because they think they've completed the Breakout activity, only to open the box and finding a pile of random pieces of text and the directions to one more activity to finish.

Let's make the clue! I'd like students to find a bunch of tiny slips of paper, each with a random number printed on them. ONE of those little slips of paper will have "AU" written on the back in UV pen – which is the periodic symbol for gold. Once they've found that symbol on the sheet of paper, they've successfully found gold and completed the activity.

To help me make these slips of paper, I can use an online random number generator (see resources at the end of the book). This will, with a little formatting in Google Docs or Microsoft Word, give us lots of random numbers that can be printed out and cut into strips or pieces.

To make this final clue VERY difficult, I could, in addition to my random number slips, take random strips of paper from the recycle bin, cut them into similar strips and sizes, and add them into the mix. In either case, we'd suggest putting all of the little strips into a plastic sealable bag to ensure the one with "AU" doesn't accidentally slip out anywhere.

The correct number on the "AU" paper could either be given to me for verification or they could put it into a Google Form which would allow them to self-check.

Wow! That seems like a lot of work!

It may seem like a lot of work, but we now have a CUSTOM Breakout activity that corresponds EXACTLY with what we want our students to know, and what we did in class with OUR textbook.

Step Seven: Setting a story and deciding what's in the box

The next step is to set the story. This is important because, before we print clues, we'll want a western font and a "sheriff's star" on the top of each page or envelope before we print, to stay consistent with the theme. To us, nothing says "Westward expansion" like the old west - so our basic story will be "The sheriff got kidnapped! You have one hour to get the gold coins and break him out, or our town will be forever run by bandits!"

There are poster templates for every occasion and theme, if you know where to find them. "Wanted" posters (like they had in the old west) would be perfect to set the mood for this day; printing a dozen or so posters on 8.5x11" paper should cover most of a classroom door to let students know that something exciting is about to happen. To add a personal twist, use your own photo as the "bandit" that's captured the sheriff, or someone else that's highly recognizable from your school, like the principal. We used photofunia.com to generate the example below.

A fun "Old West" poster made in PhotoFunia

While we've already decided that the Breakout box will have a final activity inside, we could also, in the spirit of the gold rush, have "gold chocolate coins" ready once students complete the final puzzle. If this isn't appropriate for your classroom, find something equivalent for your students.

 Storytime with Pete:
Professionalism Counts!

"Not long ago, I was running a Breakout session with 8th grade students that I had never met or worked with before. I had their Breakout boxes prepared and gave each student their first clue in a printed envelope which I designed in Microsoft Word. I heard at least three comments from different groups saying something like, "Wow, these look so professional!" Unless you're out of printer ink/toner, students notice and appreciate the work of something that looks sharp. Hand-write clues only if you need to, as with the UV pen."

Step Eight: Print the clues and set the locks

We'll need to set the locks according to our four clues. To review, they are:

Clue #1: 124 on three-digit lock (This comes from our Morse code sound, and there's nothing to print.)

Clue #2: Down-Up-Left-Left-Up-Left on the directional lock which is PORTER. (Include the decoder for this clue.)

Clue #3: 9397 on the four-digit lock, which comes from a Google Form

Clue #4: WATER on the word lock, which comes from a printed clue

Clue #5: (In Breakout Box): Random numbers, one with "AU" written on the back in UV pen, all placed into a plastic bag.

Links to online sample clues for this activity can be found in the Resources section.

Step Nine: Practice and setup

This step is pretty self-explanatory - just make sure the locks are set and open correctly. If you have a colleague or a student at home that matches the intended age / grade level of the Breakout, feel free to run the clues by them to get feedback. Make any necessary changes.

Step Ten: Reflections and adaptations

Normally, reflection happens AFTER a Breakout, but there are some things to consider as we make clues for the Breakout:

With Clue #1: If we had different fifth graders over the course of the day and wanted to be sure that students didn't "give away" the Morse code translation, it would only take about two minutes to create a different Morse code sequence on the website - say "Code 844" instead of "Code 124" - and because three digit locks are easily resettable, we can do that in between periods.

With Clue #2: The number "1893" was when Robert Porter resigned as the head of the US Census. This would make an excellent hint card for this activity.

We use this ten-step process *every time* we create a custom Breakout experience. Although you may feel overwhelmed after reading this chapter, be reassured that as you create custom clues, the process gets easier every time.

The Breakout that we created is customized for your school and curriculum, and can be used for future years to come as a meaningful and engaging activity for your fifth grade class studying Westward expansion.

CHAPTER 8: AFTER IT'S OVER

So it's over. In your classroom there was either joy or sorrow, and almost certainly some excitement and frustration. Once you've completed the activity:

- Make sure all the locks stay OPEN at the end of the activity (for an easier teacher reset).
- If you can, give students (or teachers, if you're doing this with a faculty group) a few minutes to collect their thoughts, use the restrooms, and take a few deep breaths. Before asking for feedback on the activity, it's important to remember that the past hour or so has been high-energy, fast-paced, and both minds and hearts are racing. It's certainly appropriate to take a moment to relax and shift gears back into a classroom setting where you are firmly in control of the room.
- Fill out reflection cards or forms. New boxes purchased from BreakoutEDU now contain "feedback cards." We've seen various ways to ask for student feedback on a paper card - everything from an exit ticket with a grid of facial expressions to a Google Form with multiple pages of in-depth questions to complete. While both of

these options are good ways to get individual student feedback, we've found that the best types of reflections usually happen during a class discussion at the conclusion of the activity.

- One advantage of a reflection activity - especially in a traditional Breakout setup - is that students who finish earlier than other groups have something constructive to do. They can take their time writing about the activity as other groups finish. Classrooms using the ticketing method, with every group working to unlock a single Breakout box, can use a Google Form as a way to take a deep breath, and get back into "classroom" mode. If you don't think you'll have time for everyone to fill out the "reflection form" (or if students don't actually make their way into the box), have a quick discussion before dismissing the students.

At the end of an activity, we always ask for OPEN locks to be placed inside the box, and for paper from clues or envelopes to be placed in the trash or recycle. This gives students clear directions to clean up and reset for discussion or reflection.

After the kids leave, do a little bit of teacher self-reflection. What could change next time? Was there a clue that gave students particular trouble? Did you have to give a hint to every group about the same clue? If you're giving the same Breakout session in a future period, can you make a quick last-minute adjustment if needed?

Storytime with Pete:
2016 makes a huge difference!

"I made a clue once that said something like "In this country there are colleges a'plenty, community colleges alone number one thousand and seventy. There's one college that's more important than any of these... find the number of people in this college, if you please." I included a 3D printed map of the electoral college without Alaska and Hawaii. As these Breakout activities were during the 2016 presidential election in the United States, I figured the clue would be easily recognizable. There are normally 538 votes in the electoral college, and Alaska and Hawaii combine for 7 votes. Therefore, the answer to this particular clue was 531, which opened either a three or four digit numeric lock.

After running this clue with social studies and other teachers across several sessions at several different high schools, elementary schools, and middle schools, I noticed that teachers would continually get stuck on this clue. Often, teachers would use a hint card and I'd give them a clue like, 'Do you see Alaska or Hawaii on this map?' or 'Which college is represented here?' which would - eventually - lead teachers to the correct answer.

It wasn't until a group reflection and discussion that I understood where the sticking point was.   Most teachers eventually realized that I was talking about the electoral college, but assumed that, because I did not include Alaska or Hawaii, that this was a map of the electoral college before two states joined the union. They were therefore looking through old electoral college maps and coming up with the wrong number of votes, which led to significant frustration.   They were making the clue much harder than I originally intended for it to be.

I took a permanent marker and wrote "2016" on the back of the 3D printed electoral college maps but made no other changes to the clue wording.   I re-ran the activity with several new teacher groups and was astounded that I did not get a single request for a hint. It was still tricky, with lots of spirited discussion over what the various heights of the states could mean, but the clue took much less time which ensured that participants had a good chance of breaking out of the box."

A 3D-printed map of the US Electoral College, used as a Breakout clue

Reflections are also extremely important in the event that students don't actually "Break out" in time. While we purposefully design experiences so that students and teachers alike have a good chance of succeeding (especially at first), every so often we run a Breakout box where students and/or teachers run out of time. In our experience, this is almost always because the group refuses to ask for a hint, or if they do, it's too late for them to break out.

If a group of students does not break out, and they are asked in a separate, small-group reflection what they would do differently next time, the answer is almost always, "Ask for help sooner." We draw out the idea that it's okay to ask for help not only during a Breakout, but when they don't understand class material as well.

Finally, at the conclusion of an activity, if we come up with clues that work really well, or that we get good feedback on, we'll do our best to share those with other people on our team. In the same way, if you have a good social studies clue and you have someone else that likes to run Breakout boxes on your school's grade level team, or in your department, then share that clue with them. Google Drive, Dropbox, and Google Slides presentations are great ways to create repositories of different clues.

CHAPTER NINE: FREQUENTLY ASKED QUESTIONS

In both our workshops and on electronic discussion boards, we often see teachers that are new to Breakout boxes ask some very similar questions. We've done our best to answer the most common ones here.

"Does anyone know about a Breakout activity for my math / science / language arts / social studies / physical education unit?"

There *might* be a Breakout activity for that unit, but by the time you search through all the pre-made activities, find one that *might* fit your classroom well, and adjust the clues to match your class' ability levels, content, curriculum, student needs, technology devices and other resources, it can be tricky and time-consuming. We suggest designing your own clues to ensure that your Breakout runs smoothly.

This is similar to designing lessons for an interactive whiteboard - the SMART Exchange and Promethean Planet have some really good ideas for interactive whiteboard lessons, but it's rarely "One size fits all." You need to search for and download that lesson, modify it for use in your classroom, and then deliver it. Depending on how much work it requires, sometimes it's best just to start designing the lesson from scratch!

"My locks won't work. Is there an easy way to reset them?"

In short, no. If all locks had a "master reset" code, or an incredibly easy way to break into them, then no consumers would buy the locks since thieves would easily be able to open any store-bought lock and make off with the goods. Most locks don't have a "master code," which means you're stuck trying every possible combination.

On some locks, this isn't hard. A three digit lock, for example, only has 1,000 possible combinations. The worst case scenario is that you'll have to try each of those 1,000 combinations before you crack the lock. Put on your favorite movie, and start working through the combinations (000, 001, 002, etc.). A four digit lock has almost 10,000 combinations and will certainly take some time. At that point, you can either try 1,000 combinations a day or give it to a student as a challenge, for extra credit, or some other reward.

Other locks, like the original combination lock, have too many combinations to realistically try and should be discarded. While there are online videos that suggest various ways to try to get into these, we don't recommend any of them because **the locks will never be reliable again**. You can try all possible combinations of word locks if you have some tenacity. At some point, though, you have to ask yourself if it's worth spending 4 to 5 hours just to get a lock open again. If a lock costs $7.99 and it costs you 4 hours in time to open, you're essentially making $2 an hour. Would you do extra work at school for $2 an hour? We doubt it.

There are various digital locks available (especially for the directional lock) that will offer to back up your combination electronically. We have not had good luck with these locks. Upon ordering such locks, we found them to "stick" just as much as the original locks -- sometimes before we even cracked open the lock packaging. We can't imagine what a few rounds of "Breakout" attempts would do to them.

What do you do with unexpected lock failures the night before running a Breakout activity?

First, remember to have backup locks. (Actually, have a "backup" one of everything, including UV pens and flashlights.) We've learned to keep an extra directional lock or two on hand because those will become "bricked" the most often for us. While it's an extra $20 or so in materials, it's good insurance if we're about to run a session with teachers and don't want to run short because our locks suddenly malfunctioned.

If you're in a last-minute jam, remember that not every clue needs to open a lock. While the activity certainly works best if you have a variety of locks for students to solve, you can simply have one clue lead to another in the case of a lock failure. For example, let's say that in your Breakout, Clue #1 opens a directional lock, and Clue #2 opens a four-digit lock. The night before the activity, your directional lock breaks and you can't go out and buy another one. (Let's further assume that you can't use the BreakoutEDU Locks app on the iOS store.)

To solve this problem, just use a Google Form to re-work clue #1 so that it points to clue #2. For example, if your directional lock combination was Up-Up-Left, create a Google Form that accepts only this as the correct answer and tells your students the location of Clue #2 when they get it right.

To illustrate, before the directional lock breaks, your workflow looks like this:

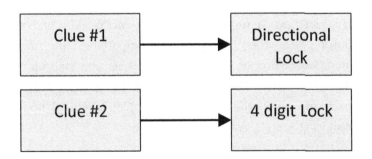

New workflow without the use of your directional lock:

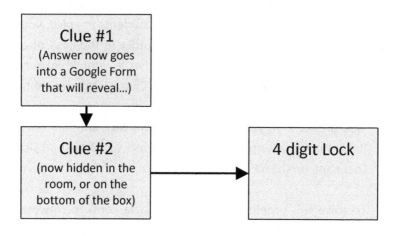

How can I raise money for Breakout boxes for my school or classroom?

If you're short on funds and your school / district won't purchase the boxes or reimburse you for the materials, your best option may be to run a creative school fundraiser.

You could have a fundraiser night at McDonalds, find a sponsor for the boxes, set something up on DonorsChoose.org, or ask your PTO to help you take up a collection. For more on this subject, we highly recommend you read our other guidebook called <u>High School Fundraising Secrets</u> available on Amazon.

What do you do about students that cheat?

Some teachers have five or six different groups of kids over the course of the day. If this is you, you'll need to find a way to differentiate the clues so that when kids talk about their awesome experience in class over lunch (along with the clues that go with it), they'll still have to solve a puzzle when they get to class that afternoon.

It should also be noted here that you've got kids voluntarily talking about school during lunch or passing periods - this means that they are engaged in your classroom, which is a good thing. Faculty members would do the same thing in the faculty lounge or cafeteria, so don't be too hard on your students. Pick a lock that's easy to change the combination to and add a subtle twist: Reverse the combination, add a random number to the 3 or 4 digit combination lock, or some other simple twist that would prevent a student in period 1 from writing down all the solutions for a student in period 2, who could have a box opened in a matter of minutes.

We've found, though, in our classrooms and in the schools that we work with, that students don't want to ruin the Breakout experience for the next group. If you ask students to be quiet about it, they usually are.

What's a DIGITAL breakout?

A digital version of a Breakout box has no physical locks to unravel. As long as you can park your students in front of computers or devices, you can run a Breakout session. Because they'll almost certainly be working in groups, you don't have to be in a 1:1 school for this to work.

For a digital Breakout experience, you don't have to print or buy *anything*. You can run the entire activity off of a single Google Form with some basic logic built in.

We recommend that you read the official BreakoutEDU guide to digital versions of a Breakout.

CHAPTER 10: FINAL THOUGHTS

Because Breakouts are a refreshing change of pace from the traditional teacher-centric classroom, and because they can be adapted to fit any grade level and topic, we're passionate about their use. They don't need to be a part of your daily or even weekly classroom routine, but they are an excellent tool for teachers to motivate and engage students, reach out to different learning styles, and challenge students to think in new ways.

Teachers are inherently creative, passionate people, and sometimes it's easy to get stuck in a routine of textbooks, worksheets, websites, and videos. Breakout boxes provide you with a way to find your creative side and show your students that you're passionate about their success. We challenge you to not rely solely on the Breakout box experiences that others have made. We know that after a little practice, you will find that it's really not that hard to make your own custom Breakout experiences for your students.

We knew that custom Breakouts were something special after running a session in a second grade classroom in suburban Chicago. We created a custom Breakout review for a second grade class that involved math, language, social studies, and science, and were amazed at the response. Students joyfully shared their excitement with us, and asked us when we would be back to do another Breakout activity.

After our session in that second grade classroom, the "Breakout idea" spread quickly throughout the school. Other faculty members reached out to us wanting to know more. The middle school gifted teacher and her students took action. After introducing the Breakout box and completing an activity with her class, the students designed a custom box for their classmates to solve. Other grades followed, and within a few weeks, Breakout boxes were commonplace for students at the school.

We hope that this book guides you, inspires you, encourages you and supports you -- whether you're about to start your first Breakout or whether you're experienced and looking for deeper curriculum integration! We've shared the Breakout experience with students and teachers across the country, and we constantly see teachers pushing the envelope with their creativity. We're excited to see what you come up with! So, our final note to you:

We'd love to hear your story. Reach out to us if you've got a Breakout experience that you'd like to share.

You can reach us at Haley@BreakoutsMadeEasy.com or Pete@BreakoutsMadeEasy.com

Good luck with your Breakouts!

RESOURCES

For your convenience, we've included this list of the tools and recommendations used throughout this guide. Please keep in mind these are subject to change.

Bit.ly: A website that allows you to shorten URLs using the Bit.ly domain as the link.

BreakoutEDU.com: BreakoutEDU.com is a resource for free, pre-made games available in the BreakoutEDU community (see BreakoutEDU.com/beta). In addition, you may purchase all materials you need for a Breakout via BreakoutEDU.com.

BreakoutEDU.com/beta: To receive access to the free, pre-made games available in the BreakoutEDU community, you must register as a BreakoutEDU beta tester. During this free signup, you will need to provide a little information about yourself such as your name and email.

BreakoutsMadeEasy.com: Haley and Pete's website designed to support *Breakouts Made Easy* readers. You'll find additional resources here as we have the time to add them.

Clues for the Westward Expansion example:
goo.gl/M24OCZ

Crosswordlabs.com: A free, online printable crossword generator to use as one of your clues within your custom made Breakout. (They also work well for hint cards, or in combination with other problems.)

Dafont.com: A free collection of downloadable fonts to help make clues match your Breakout theme.

Directional Decoder Key: Used to translate a word solution into a directional lock combination. You can use this same idea to translate letters to numbers, directions to numbers, etc. By using a decoder key, you can make any clue fit any lock.

Find our copy of this here: goo.gl/yGhftk

DonorsChoose.org: Teachers can set up a quick page here and petition others to fund their classroom Breakout boxes (or any other supplies your classroom might need). Check their website for conditions and details.

Dropbox: A free, easy way to share files with other people, similar to Google Drive.

E.ggtimer.com: A quick, full-screen countdown timer we like to use during our Breakouts. It's clean, simple and gets the job done. However, keep in mind that e.ggtimer.com requires Internet access.

Flaticon.com: Icons used throughout this book are from Freepik at flaticon.com.

Forms.google.com: A tool that is part of the Google Suite for Education for creating surveys, tests, or input forms. We use Google forms to create easy clues using data validation.

Google Drive: Login to Google to access, store, and share files anywhere through secure cloud storage.

Goo.gl: A website that allows you to shorten and simplify URL links; designed and supported by Google.

http://morsecode.scphillips.com/translator.html: A free Morse Code Translator that will convert typed text into the short and long "beeps" of Morse code.

http://www.history.com/topics/gold-rush-of-1849:
A video and article about the Gold Rush. We used this to create an example clue when designing a Breakout about Western Expansion.

https://commons.wikimedia.org/wiki/File:Pigpen.png: A link to the "Pig Pen Cipher". We use this as an example of a cipher to include in your custom Breakout.

http://www.pangloss.com/seidel/rnumber.cgi: A website that generates random numbers that can be printed out and cut into strips or pieces for a Breakout clue.

Jigsawplanet.com: An online resource used as an alternative to physical hand-cut puzzle pieces. We suggest this website for clues because it works well on all devices and so physical puzzle pieces don't get lost or misplaced.

K5Learning.com: Offers a wide variety of online practice worksheets for free.

Keepvid.com: Used to download a local copy of videos on your laptop or Chromebook so that in case of a lost Internet connection, the video can still be used in your Breakout and saved for later use.

LOCKS app by BreakoutEDU: An iOS app developed by the BreakoutEDU team so that you don't need to buy boxes, locks, replacement locks, more replacement locks, etc. There are unique virtual locks in the app, like the color lock, that don't have a physical lock equivalent.

Photofunia.com: Used to create real-looking "wanted posters," secret agent files, and dozens of other great photos for use in a Breakout activity.

THE QR Code Extension: Used on Chromebooks to scan QR codes; found on the Google Chrome web store.

Qrcode.kaywa.com: Used to create printable QR codes.

Qrstuff.com: Used to create printable QR codes.

Scribblemaps.com: Used to create and share maps with symbols, markers, and a distance measurement tool.

Tinkercad.com: A free, online design studio to create three-dimensional objects.

Tinyurl.com: A free service to make long URLs customized and shortened.

Wordlock Combinations: Find sample word combinations at wordlock.com/_pdf/Wordlock-Padlock-Instructions.pdf

Made in the USA
Monee, IL
11 March 2021